QuoteOctopus.com

The best quotes

Publisher Contact

257 Swanston Street, Melbourne, VIC, AUSTRALIA

Email: hello@quoteoctopus.com

Social media: facebook.com/quoteoctopus

Acknowledgements

The team at Quote Octopus would like to thank our friends, family, suppliers and customers for making our vision of creating the highest-quality books a reality. Thanks for purchasing and enjoy the quotes!

This page is intentionally left blank

This page is intentionally left blank

'Santa Sangre' is the picture I love the best, myself, because 'El Topo' and 'The Holy Mountain' I made with my head, and 'Santa Sangre' I made with my feelings, with my heart. It's an emotional picture. And it's more real for me, that picture.

Alejandro Jodorowsky

A man doesn't cry. In my life, I've never cried. I cannot do it. I am a man. How will I cry?

Alejandro Jodorowsky

A person is not the same in his life at all times. Your consciousness is developing all the time. When I started making 'El Topo,' I was one person. When I finished that picture, I was another person.

Alejandro Jodorowsky

A true artist is always out of his time.

Alejandro Jodorowsky

Accepting death is a massive problem for everybody.

Alejandro Jodorowsky

All my life, I have never found a person who really loved this world. Every person hates the world, how he is.

Alejandro Jodorowsky

All the pictures I could never do, I'll do it in comics. All the comics I do are the pictures I could never do.

Alejandro Jodorowsky

Being essentially a creator, I never set out to shock, always thinking about creating my work and not about the benefits it could produce.

Alejandro Jodorowsky

Birds born in cages think that flying is a disease.

Alejandro Jodorowsky

Books are finished.

Alejandro Jodorowsky

Don't make your living with cinema because Hollywood will take you, will eat you, will destroy you. This is the reality. You have a good picture, have success, you take the person and they destroy you.

Alejandro Jodorowsky

Every one of us is a perfect human being, deformed by the family, the society and the culture.

Alejandro Jodorowsky

Every person, every artist makes his life an artwork.

Alejandro Jodorowsky

Every work of art belongs to his time. I would not paint again the Mona Lisa in the third dimension.

Alejandro Jodorowsky

Failure doesn't exist. It's only a change of direction.

Alejandro Jodorowsky

Five cats and a woman. That is all I need in life.

Alejandro Jodorowsky

For me 'Dune' was a dream - a big dream!

Alejandro Jodorowsky

For me they are no different, reality and dreams.

Alejandro Jodorowsky

For me, surrealism is in my blood; it's not an effort.

Alejandro Jodorowsky

George Harrison wanted to play the thief in 'Holy Mountain.'

Alejandro Jodorowsky

Human society has dense borders - economic, religious and cultural - inculcated from an early age. We hate change.

Alejandro Jodorowsky

I always think that art is a form of sacrifice.

Alejandro Jodorowsky

I am a poet; I am not a worker. I need to be free.

Alejandro Jodorowsky

I am an artist, you understand? For me, a picture is like poetry. When you make art, this is not coming from an intellectual place. It's coming from the deep side of your unconscious, your soul.

Alejandro Jodorowsky

I am like the rain: I go where I'm needed.

Alejandro Jodorowsky

I am not a commercial industry creator. I don't believe in making art to make money.

Alejandro Jodorowsky

I am not a man. I am not a human being inside. I am not that. I don't know what I am, but I am not that.

Alejandro Jodorowsky

I am not a normal person. I am living in a normal body, but my mind is not normal.

Alejandro Jodorowsky

I am not like Hitchcock, directing the reaction of the public or the audience. I don't like that. I think this is some kind of fascism - 'You need to react like that.' No. No. It's not like this; everyone needs to react as he can.

Alejandro Jodorowsky

I am still radical!

Alejandro Jodorowsky

I believe in mysticism, with an interior goal, and you are your own temple and your own priest. I don't believe anymore in religions, because you see today there are religious wars, prejudice, false morals, and the woman is despised. Religion is too old now; it's from another century, it's not for today.

Alejandro Jodorowsky

I didn't want to make cinema so a person forgets himself and has a lot of fun. 'I forget myself, I am a little poor consumer.' I wanted to make a picture where someone who sees it say, 'This is me! This is me!'

Alejandro Jodorowsky

I don't believe in failing. I have dignity.

Alejandro Jodorowsky

I don't live in France; I live in myself.

Alejandro Jodorowsky

I don't regret any past. I am not there. I am not sorry not to make pictures, because I know one day I will do it. I intend to live 150 years.

Alejandro Jodorowsky

I don't see myself as a moviemaker only, you know? When I can do a picture, I do. But I don't work like a business, in pictures. I am not obliged to make one picture after the other in order to live.

Alejandro Jodorowsky

I don't want to just love my family; I want to love all of humanity.

Alejandro Jodorowsky

I feel terrible for directors of TV because all the episodes have to look the same. They make a great series for five or six years, and then when it's canceled, they can't break out on their own.

Alejandro Jodorowsky

I grew up in the north of Chile, and this is why there are a lot of religious symbols in my pictures: because the Catholic Church in Latin America is very strong.

Alejandro Jodorowsky

I had a big problem working with stars, because they are too expensive and have too many demands. Their names help you raise the money to make the movie, but then they demand close-ups. They change things. You end up doing things at their service instead of servicing the film.

Alejandro Jodorowsky

I hated Peter O'Toole. I wanted to kill that guy! When they said he was dead, I was happy. People said, 'Poor Peter O'Toole.' I was happy!

Alejandro Jodorowsky

I have always thought that, of all the arts, the cinema is the most complete art.

Alejandro Jodorowsky

I like Hollywood movies. I like them like I like to eat scrambled eggs; I like them for fun.

Alejandro Jodorowsky

I liked Lady Gaga's meat dress. It was funny.

Alejandro Jodorowsky

I live making comics. Comics is an industrial art but less suffering, because comics are for young people who are more adventurous. I do that. I live off comics, and then I write books, but when you want movies, you cannot make movies without money.

Alejandro Jodorowsky

I never wanted to study art. And I don't think you need to study art if you are an artist. It's even dangerous to go to school. You need to do whatever you want, as you want.

Alejandro Jodorowsky

I say, 'If somebody steals something of yours, then it's good; he loves what you do.'

Alejandro Jodorowsky

I tweet 15 times a day to keep my brain stimulated.

Alejandro Jodorowsky

I want to liberate my imagination and my mind with every kind of movie. That is what I wanted to do all my life.

Alejandro Jodorowsky

I wanted to be loved by my father. I could do anything to be loved by my father.

Alejandro Jodorowsky

I was a happy man, never working. Sometimes I saw days with no money to eat. It was not so difficult.

Alejandro Jodorowsky

I was alone as a child. I lived in fairytales, adventures, Shakespeare. They are the friends, my books.

Alejandro Jodorowsky

I was like a mutant when I was a boy. I learned to read when I was four years old; it was like a miracle.

Alejandro Jodorowsky

I write books, I write for comic books, I give lectures... I live. And when the opportunity comes to do a picture, I do a picture.

Alejandro Jodorowsky

I've seen 'Hamlet' many times, and Hamlet, he was just a hideous neurotic; he never changes. He doubts - all the way to the end, all the way until when he dies, he doubts.

Alejandro Jodorowsky

If God gives you chocolate, you open your mouth, no?

Alejandro Jodorowsky

If you are great, 'El Topo' is a great picture. If you are limited, 'El Topo' is limited.

Alejandro Jodorowsky

If you don't make errors, how can you be conscious?

Alejandro Jodorowsky

In Chile, they have no movies. They have awful popular movies.

Alejandro Jodorowsky

In Mexico, when we want to speak deep secrets, we drink pulgue together. It is a drink made from the cactus plant, and when you take the bottle from your mouth, it leaves a string behind, between the mouth and the bottle, like a spider's web. It shows that the truth sticks inside.

Alejandro Jodorowsky

In history, psychedelic plants were used by priests and shamans with a desire to discover the interior.

Alejandro Jodorowsky

In movies, images cost - if you want a big image, it takes more money.

Alejandro Jodorowsky

In order to be something, you must do something.

Alejandro Jodorowsky

It's not the same thing to make a work - a film, a book, a play - about youth as it is to make one about old age.

Alejandro Jodorowsky

It's so weird to be alive and to be inside a body.

Alejandro Jodorowsky

Lady Gaga has a lot of energy, and that is fantastic, but she is using old surrealist images.

Alejandro Jodorowsky

Let the inner god that is in each one of us speak. The temple is your body, and the priest is your heart: it is from here that every awareness must begin.

Alejandro Jodorowsky

Life is a mixing of all kind of things: comedy and tragedy going together.

Alejandro Jodorowsky

Life is beautiful, what do you think? In the morning I say, 'Ah, I am alive still!' All my friends die already. I am alive. It is fantastic.

Alejandro Jodorowsky

Maybe I am a prophet. I really hope one day there will come Confucius, Muhammad, Buddha and Christ to see me. And we will sit at a table, taking tea and eating some brownies.

Alejandro Jodorowsky

Movies have an enormous power to open the mind and the heart and everything.

Alejandro Jodorowsky

My consciousness is without limits more than when I was 40 or 50.

Alejandro Jodorowsky

My ego every day is more and more polite. I tame it.

Alejandro Jodorowsky

My father was a monster. A monster! I cut with my family when I was 23 and I never see them again.

Alejandro Jodorowsky

My father was an atheist, absent. He was a salesman; I was four years old when he told me that the end of life was death.

Alejandro Jodorowsky

My films are completely new. I am not similar to anybody in the history of movies.

Alejandro Jodorowsky

My films are like clouds: their meaning keeps changing every minute.

Alejandro Jodorowsky

My grandfather was a very mystical guy who travelled from Argentina to Chile, across the mountains with a donkey, carrying the Torah.

Alejandro Jodorowsky

My ideal audience is on the young side, eager to mutate and move to a higher level of consciousness. I want my images to turn the viewer's brain into what it is: a flying carpet.

Alejandro Jodorowsky

My second wife, the mother of one of my sons, died of murder. I was not with her, but I could have saved her. I think.

Alejandro Jodorowsky

My wife is 37 years younger than me. I don't feel the difference.

Alejandro Jodorowsky

Normality is to be different. Every person is a different person. And one day you need to be aware of your difference. Aware that you are not the same as the others. That is to be normal.

Alejandro Jodorowsky

One day I was sitting in my own pain, and suddenly all the pain and troubles of the world came to me. I received all the pain of the world, all through my body.

Alejandro Jodorowsky

People say I am mad. I am not mad. I am trying to heal my soul.

Alejandro Jodorowsky

Pretty soon we will no longer have movies. We will have television series only.

Alejandro Jodorowsky

Psychoanalysis wants to heal with words and speaking, but sometimes with speaking, you realize nothing.

Alejandro Jodorowsky

Revolutions are of no us;, it is necessary to work on transforming the brain: on sowing a different knowledge/awareness, on creating a new conscience, that is like a magic box full of brains.

Alejandro Jodorowsky

Scientific thought and the miraculous unconscious are two waves in the same ocean.

Alejandro Jodorowsky

Society feeds terror and is in turn terrorized; we are afraid to lose, so we consume.

Alejandro Jodorowsky

Surrealism - in particular with Salvador Dali - was all about ego. It was all about extreme individualism.

Alejandro Jodorowsky

Surrealism was necessary - essential, even - in the 1920s to bridge the gap between rationalism and the subconscious. It started something important. But by the early '60s, it had become petit-bourgeois; it was too intellectual and romantic, and had ground to a halt. It had become respectable.

Alejandro Jodorowsky

Tarantino's 'Django' amused me very much. It is as made by an adult that was still a child.

Alejandro Jodorowsky

The Arabs have a God, the Jews have another, and the Catholics have another! And they're all fighting to maintain that they worship the one real God. Idiots!

Alejandro Jodorowsky

The end of the surrealism movement was so political, so artistically pure.

Alejandro Jodorowsky

The first thing I didn't understand was my life. It's a mystery. And today I don't understand economy or politics. I don't know why politics or economy are destroying the world, but I will understand after understanding.

Alejandro Jodorowsky

The planet is ill, everyone knows that. But I need to be optimistic, otherwise I would just be adding to the negativity. So every night I come on Madrid TV and read a piece of good news.

Alejandro Jodorowsky

The tarot is sacred.

Alejandro Jodorowsky

The world is not violent. But there is a lot of violence in it.

Alejandro Jodorowsky

The worse the newspapers speak of the world, the better I feel.

Alejandro Jodorowsky

To be an artist, you need to play inside your work.

Alejandro Jodorowsky

To have hands, to have fingers, is weird. Real life is weird, to have fingers?

Alejandro Jodorowsky

Today a picture has value if it makes a lot of money. Myself, I declare I want to make a picture to lose money. Really! I want to lose money.

Alejandro Jodorowsky

We all exist in our own personal reality of craziness.

Alejandro Jodorowsky

We are all working for the immortality of the human consciousness.

Alejandro Jodorowsky

We have to be very conscious of the fact that beneath every illness is a prohibition. A prohibition that comes from a superstition.

Alejandro Jodorowsky

When I brought 'El Topo' to New York, no one understood the picture. But John Lennon understood. John and Yoko Ono, they presented 'El Topo' in the United States; they introduced it.

Alejandro Jodorowsky

When I started to pay income tax, I was 50 years old.

Alejandro Jodorowsky

When I was a young person I went to the university and I learned a rational language, to think with the left side of the brain. But in the right side of the brain you have intuition and imagination. Words are not the truth; they indicate the way to go, but you need to go alone, in silence. Symbols have a language that kills the words.

Alejandro Jodorowsky

When I was an adolescent, I abandoned my country at 23 years to come to Paris to know Andre Breton, the 'Pope of Surrealism.' And for three years, I was there working with him being a surrealist.

Alejandro Jodorowsky

When I'm not creating something, I get bored; I despair.

Alejandro Jodorowsky

When I'm tired, I see industrial pictures. But I'll see one every two months. If I see one every day, I'll become an idiot.

Alejandro Jodorowsky

When my father died, I did not cry. When my cat died three days later, I cried a lot.

Alejandro Jodorowsky

When you put a great amount of energy and hope in a big project, you can be destroyed if you don't do it.

Alejandro Jodorowsky

You dream every night. Every person in the world, even if they don't remember, is dreaming every night.

Alejandro Jodorowsky

You live in the image you have of the world. Every one of us lives in a different world, with different space and different time.

Alejandro Jodorowsky

This page is intentionally left blank

This page is intentionally left blank

This page is intentionally left blank

This page is intentionally left blank

This page is intentionally left blank